KNOW ALL ABOUT

Spelling

ACTIVITY BOOK

Written by Nicola Baxter

Illustrated by Natascha Nazarova

CONTENTS

What's in a word?

The good news is that every word in the English language can be written using just 26 letters. All you need to know is which letters to choose and the order to put them in!

There are two kinds of letters in the alphabet.

Remember!

Most letters of the alphabet are **consonants**:

b c d f g h j k l m n p q r s t v w x z

Five letters of the alphabet are **vowels**: **a e i o u**

One letter, **y**, can be both a vowel and a consonant. It is usually a consonant if it comes at the **beginning** of a word and a vowel if it comes anywhere else.

Every **word** must have **at least one vowel**.

1 Write each of these words in the correct list.

music useful player orchestra injury yell annoy stage edge over xylophone

Beginning with a consonant	Beginning with a vowel
. . . .
. . . .
. . . .
. . . .
. . . .
. . . .

2 Underline the vowels in these words. There may be more than one. How many did you underline altogether?

try   yellow   beat
cymbal   conductor
like   straight
drummer

Syllables

Will you practise more often?

No!
BOOM!

The way that a word sounds doesn't always tell you how to spell it correctly, but it can give some useful clues.

Sometimes it's helpful to think of words as if they were drumbeats. A short word, such as **no**, is like one drumbeat. It has one **syllable**.

Other words, such as **maybe**, are like two drumbeats. They have two syllables.

May-be!
BOOM! BOOM!

Certainly has three syllables.

Cer-tain-ly!
BOOM! BOOM! BOOM!

Every **syllable** must have **at least one vowel**.

Sometimes breaking a word down into syllables can help you to spell it.

3 Write the names of the instruments in the correct list.

flute piano trumpet trombone drum oboe triangle recorder horn guitar harp saxophone

One syllable	Two syllables	Three syllables
. . . .
. . . .
. . . .
. . . .

4 Join up one syllable from each list to make six words of three syllables, then underline the vowel or vowels in each syllable.

un	duct	ment
re	joy	or
en	e	stand
tel	play	ing
con	der	ful
dis	gret	phone

For more about consonants, vowels and syllables, look at page 4 of your Mini Reference Book

► short vowel sounds
► long vowel sounds
► spellings

Vowel sounds

Each of the five vowels (or six including **y**) can make different sounds. Sometimes this depends on which other letters are with it.

a can have a short sound:
or a long sound:

and flat mangle
ape hay stable wail

e can have a short sound:
or a long sound:

then length spent
eel seal brief theme

i can have a short sound:
or a long sound:

blink imp stick
item night climb time

o can have a short sound:
or a long sound:

stop long off
oat wrote blow gloat

u can have a short sound:
or a long sound:

cut up plunge
usual huge rule dune

y can have a short **i** sound:
or a long **i** sound:
or, at the end of a word,
a long **e** sound:

gymnast rhythm cymbal
why rhyme try

happy merry hardly

The long vowel sounds are the same as their names in the alphabet.

You will notice that there are lots of different ways of spelling the **same** vowel sound.

These are not the **only** sounds that vowels can make. Combining vowels with each other or consonants can make different sounds.

1 Put a ring round each syllable with a long vowel sound and underline each syllable with a short vowel sound.

I hate that stupid cat!

It wakes me up by scratching on my window.

I am not happy.

I will let him in right this second.

I need my sleep!

2 Put each of these words in the right drawer of the filing cabinet.

moan   screech   blow
ring   cry   whine
tune   hit   stop
scream   hum   wail
bang   play   clash
yell   pluck   use
test   song

Long a sound	Long e sound	Long i sound	Long o sound	Long u sound

Short a sound	Short e sound	Short i sound	Short o sound	Short u sound

3 These eight words have a long **a** sound in the middle. Can you find them in the wordsearch square? Notice that the long **a** sound can be spelt in several different ways.

gale
play
race
rail
stage
straight
taste
weight

```
S  T  A  G  E  E  Z  S
O  T  P  D  A  A  M  I
T  Y  R  F  O  L  S  Q
A  U  R  A  C  E  E  V
S  P  U  A  I  B  C  H
T  M  W  E  I  G  H  T
E  N  R  O  Z  L  H  D
P  L  A  Y  C  M  Q  T
```

4 Write out this poem on a separate piece of paper, choosing words with a long **i** sound from the list below.

sight   night
cried   fright
right   plight
climbed   white
might

In the middle of the ....,
The singer woke and had a ....
Her face turned ....;
Her hair was a ....;
She screamed and .... with all her ....
When she .... out of bed,
The shadow fled!
Some were sorry for her ....,
But others thought it served her ....!

Remember, just listening to the sound of a word can't tell you how it is spelt but it can give you useful clues.

For more about vowel sounds, look at page 5 of your Mini Reference Book

5

Prefixes and suffixes

If you look carefully at words, you will see that many of them are related to one another.

Start with a simple word:	view	This is called a **root** word.
You can add a group of letters to the beginning of the root:	**inter**view	This is called a **prefix**.
You can add a group of letters to the end of the root:	view**er** view**ing** view**ed**	This is called a **suffix**.
Or you can add both a prefix and a suffix:	**inter**view**er**	

1 Write a root word from the list between each pair of prefixes and suffixes to make a real word each time.

a	pro	....	er
b	ex	....	ing
c	un	....	ed
d	re	....	ment

Root words:
lock
test
port
place

Prefixes

Adding a prefix changes the meaning of the root word. Look at page 6 of your Mini Reference Book for common prefixes and their meanings.

Here are a few more:

ante means *before*   anteroom, antenatal
auto means *self*   autobiography, autograph
extra means *outside*   extraordinary, extraterrestrial
post means *after*   postmortem, postscript
sub means *under*   submarine, submerge
super means *above* or *more than*   supervisor, supermarket

Remember!

There are several different prefixes that mean *not* or *in reverse* or *opposite to*. They change a word to its opposite.

de defuse, defrost
dis disappear, dishonest
in incorrect, inexcusable
un unusual, unfortunate

The prefix and the root word do not change or lose any letters when they are joined together.

This rule means that if the last letter of the prefix and the first letter of the root word are the same, there will be a double letter.

un+named = unnamed
dis+similar = dissimilar

2 Write **de**, **dis**, **in** or **un** before each of these words to form its opposite. Remember not to lose any letters when you join the two parts together.

a trust . . . .

b forgettable . . . .

c noticed . . . .

d cipher . . . .

e dependent . . . .

3 Write **de**, **dis**, **in** or **un** before the underlined words to show what the conductor **meant** to say.

"We have been practising for an _____ <u>acceptably</u> long time," cried the conductor. "And still the music is _____ <u>bearable</u>. I am very _____ <u>satisfied</u>. Your playing is _____ <u>excusable</u>. The whole audience will _____ <u>like</u> this _____ <u>graceful</u> noise! It is _____ <u>convenient</u> for me to rehearse any longer. I am _____ <u>sure</u> whether you can improve. If you cannot, I will _____ <u>own</u> you!"

▶▶▶ MR   For more about prefixes, look at page 6 of your Mini Reference Book

Suffixes

When suffixes are added to a root word, they can change the meaning of the word or the way that it can be used.

music
musi**cian**
music**al**

Look at page 7 of your Mini Reference Book to see how suffixes can change root words into nouns, adjectives, verbs and adverbs.

You may have noticed that sometimes the spelling of the end of a root word changes a little when a suffix is added. The rules about this are easy to remember.

No change
If the root word **ends with a consonant** and the suffix **begins with a consonant**, all you have to do is join them together.

kind + ness = kindness   child + hood = childhood

Doubling
If the root word **ends with a consonant** and the suffix **begins with a vowel** (including **y**), you may need to double the consonant before you add the suffix. Just ask yourself:

Does the **last syllable** of the root word have a **short vowel sound**?

Does it **end** with a **single consonant**?

If the answer to both questions is "yes", double the consonant!
If one or both of the answers are "no", the consonant stays single.

*I was **short** and **single** until I discovered the **double** bass!*

4 Write these root words and suffixes as single words, using the rules above to decide if the last letter of the root word needs to be doubled.

a   art + ist = ...

b   child + like = ...

c   temperament + al = ...

d   drum + ing = ...

e   thump + ing = ...

All I ask is politeness!

It's outrageous!

Silent e

If the root word ends in a silent **e** and the suffix begins with a **consonant**, the root word does not change.

If the root word ends in a silent **e** and the suffix begins with a **vowel**, drop the **e**.

tremble + ing = trembling
nerve + ous = nervous

Exceptions If the root word ends with the soft sounds **ce** or **ge** and the suffix begins with **a** or **o**, don't drop the **e**. (For more about soft **c** and **g**, see pages 12–13.)

5 On a separate piece of paper write out each root word three times, adding a new suffix each time.

a notice (ed, able, ing)	**d** please (ing, ant, ed)
b tune (er, ful, ed)	**e** close (ness, ly, ing)
c serve (ice, ant, ing)	**f** place (ed, ing, ment)

Words ending in y

A root word ending in **y** does not change when you add **ing**.

try + ing = trying
worry + ing = worrying

If the root word ends in a **vowel** followed by **y**, there is no change when you add any other suffix.

play + er = player
enjoy + ment = enjoyment

Exceptions A few common one-syllable root words change the **y** to **i**. You probably already know these exceptions by sight:

pay + ed = paid   lay + ed = laid   day + ly = daily   gay + ly = gaily

Happiness is silence...

If the root word ends with a **consonant** followed by a **y**, change the **y** to **i** before all suffixes except **ing**.

ed
ly
ing
ful

6 On a separate piece of paper, write out this passage again, adding suffixes from the list to fill the gaps. Be sure to change the end of the root word if necessary.

"You are play...... too quick......!" cry...... the conductor. "I have been move...... my baton clear...... but you have been ignore...... me! This is disgrace......! At this rate, we could easy...... finish the concert before the audience has arrive......."

For more about suffixes, look at pages 6-7 of your Mini Reference Book

▶ ch/tch, ge/dge
▶ ff, ll, ss and le
▶ soft c and g

Helpful vowel sounds

Fetch me my notes! It is time for my speech!

When you are thinking about how to spell a word, the vowel sounds can give you some useful clues.

Screech and scratch

A **ch** sound in a word may be spelt **ch** or **tch**.
After a single vowel making a **short vowel sound**, use **tch**.
After a **long vowel sound** or after a **consonant**, use **ch**.

Exceptions rich such much which

1 Fill in each gap in the newspaper article with **ch** or **tch**.

> By the time he had rea......ed the end of his spee......,
> the conductor had caused su...... boredom that mu......
> of the audience had mar......ed to the door. The speaker
> tried to ca...... their attention by scree......ing more
> loudly, whi...... made him lose his voice. The wre......ed
> man is recovering on the bea....... .

Stage and edge

After a **short vowel sound**, use **dge**.
After a **long vowel sound** or after a **consonant**, use **ge**.

Exceptions
vegetable
pigeon

2 Fill in each gap with a word that rhymes with the word in brackets.

a The boat sailed under the . . . . (ridge)

b The birds built a nest in the . . . . (sedge)

c The conductor climbed on to the . . . . (page)

d Are you ready to take the . . . . ? (lunge)

e She is dreaming of a tall, dark . . . . (ranger)

Tell the boss off !

The letters **f**, **l** and **s** are always doubled when they come at the end of a word with one syllable and a short vowel.

Exceptions
bus, if, until, yes, of, is

3 Add **f**, **l** or **s** or **ff**, **ll** or **ss** to the ends of these words.

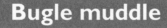

a roo____	**b** be____	**c** mo____
d spe____	**e** le____	**f** gri____
g stu____	**h** cli____	**i** mai____
j coo____	**k** loa____	**l** dre____

Bugle muddle

Usually if you hear an **el** or **ul** sound at the end of a word, it is spelt **le**.

If the word has a single vowel making a short sound, there must be two consonants before the **le**. If you only hear one consonant sound, it must be a double letter.

If the word already has two consonants after the vowel or has a long vowel sound, there is no need for doubling.

Exceptions A few common words end with **el** or **al**.

towel   tunnel   label   travel   model   channel   flannel
medal   cymbal   pedal   metal

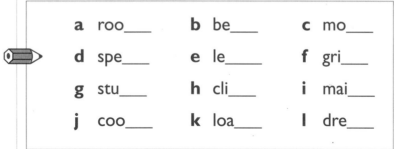

It's a struggle!

It's simple!

You're feeble!

4 Put **le** in each gap, doubling the letter before it if necessary.

The tab____ had such a wob_____ that the nood_____s tumb____d on to the floor. "I'll hand____ this!" bab_____d the drummer. But he stumb____d with the ket_____ and was unab____ to stay on his feet. "What a mud_____!" he grumb_____d.

▶▶▶ MR   **For more about vowel sounds, look at pages 10–12 of your Mini Reference Book**

I feel sick!

Why don't you think before you speak?

Take that back!

A hard **c** sound at the end of a word is usually spelt **k**, **ke** or **ck**.

Use **ck** immediately after a short vowel.

ck is never used after a long vowel sound or when there is another consonant before the **k** sound.

When a word ends with an **ic** (hard) sound, this is always spelt **ick** in a word with one syllable but **ic** in a word with more than one syllable.

5 Fill in **ic** or **ick** in the gaps in the words on the poster.

Fantast......!

Mag......!

Histor...... event!

Gigant...... talent!

P...... up your t......ets here!

Hard and soft c and g

The letter **c** becomes a soft **s** sound and the letter **g** becomes a soft **j** sound before **e**, **i** or **y**.

ceiling   centre   circle   circus   cycle
germ   giant   magic   engine   gymnast

Exceptions Some very common words don't follow the hard **g** rule. You probably know them already.

get   girl
gift

6 Put an **e**, **i** or **y** in each of these words.

a c...ntre **b** bic...cle **c** c...nema **d** c...ntipede

e c...mbal **f** g...nger **g** g...raffe **h** g...mnasium

*Wait **just** a minute!*

If a word sounds as though it begins with a hard **c** followed by an **e**, **i** or **y** sound, it must begin with a **k**.

kitchen keep

If a word begins with a soft **g** sound followed by an **a**, **o** or **u** sound, use a **j**.

Exceptions to the soft **g** or **j** rule:

jelly jest jeans jeer jet jewel jingle

I was only joking!

7 Fill the gaps with the correct letter to make a hard **c** sound.

...ome here my little ...itty ...at! Mummy wants to give you a ...iss and a ...uddle.

This is the ...ind of thing I ...annot ...ope with!

8 Fill in the gaps with a **k** or a **c**.

...an you ...eep a secret?

Of ...ourse!

I've re...ently been told that the ...on...ert may be ...an...elled!

Who will de...ide?

The ...onductor. He's lost his voi...e again.

9 The letters making the soft **g** sounds in these words have been missed out. Fill each gap with a **g** or a **j**.

Which ...oker has taken my ...ar of royal ...elly?

...ust a ...ot, ...ently applied, ...enerally makes a ...igantic improvement to my ...awline.

The ...entleman who invented it was a ...enius!

More long vowel sounds

I say! May I play on Friday?

As you know, long vowel sounds are often spelt with a silent **e** at the end of the word or with two vowels together. Here are some other useful spellings that you have already seen on pages 4 and 5.

Long a

A long **a** sound at the end of a word is spelt **ay**.

I Fill in the long **a** sounds in the double bass player's song.

I'm going aw......	But this I'll s......,
On holid...... .	Throughout my st......,
I don't fear r......n	From Saturd......
In sunny Sp......n.	To Wednesd......
I'll lie all d......	I WILL NOT PL......!
In a sandy b...... .	

Long i

Before a **t**, a long **i** might be spelt **igh**.

Can this be right? A light at night? You gave me a fright!

Long o

A long **o** sound at the end of a word is usually spelt **ow**.

Exceptions some short words end with **oe** and a few common words just end in **o**.

Show me the way to blow.

toe hoe foe

no so to potato piano tomato zero hero soprano

2 Fill in the gaps with **ow**, **o** or **oe**.

I wanted t...... sh...... the sopran...... that I was a her......, s...... I tried t...... lift the pian.......

I don't kn...... what t...... say

My lift was sl....... My cheeks began to gl.......

Did you succeed?

N......! I dropped it on her t......!

3 The violinist is not very good at spelling. She has had two attempts at several words. Cross out the spelling that you think is wrong. Then write out the whole letter correctly on a separate sheet of paper.

Dear Sir,

I am writting/writing to/too you as I do not think I am beeing/being payed/paid enough. I shoed/showed my uncle/unckle hoe/how mutch/much I am earning and he was shoked/shocked. We would not have to et/eat noddles/noodles if we earned a desent/decent wage/waje.

Yours truly/truely

I. M. A. Bower

MR ▶▶▶ For more about long vowel sounds, look at pages 5 and 12 of your Mini Reference Book

Silent letters

*There's no si**gn** of the conductor.*

*Do you **kn**ow where he is?*

*Li**st**en! Here's a story I've **wr**itten.*

Some words have silent letters. You can't hear them when you say the word. Look carefully at the words and pictures below and you will soon find it easy to remember the most common ones.

g before n

Sometimes the letter **g** is silent before **n**:

gnat gnaw gnome sign
reign foreign campaign

1 Fill each of the gaps with **ng** or **gn**.

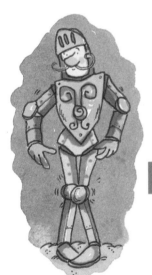

Lo...... ago, in the rei...... of Ki...... John, a forei......
ki.....dom began a campai...... against him. The first
si...... of anythi...... bei...... wro...... came when the
Ki...... was stu...... by a swarm of sti......i......
......ats. One day a stra......er came to the Ki......'s aid.

k before n

These common words sound as though they begin with **n** but there is a silent **k** at the beginning.

knot know knew knees
kneel knife knickers
knight knob knock

2 Fill in each gap with a silent **k** word from the list above.

"I .... that I should .... before a
king," said the ...., "but in this armour, my
.... hit the ground with such a ...., it's
as though a .... is going through them."

t after s

t cannot usually be heard when it follows **s** in the middle of a word.

castle whistle bristle
thistle rustle bustle listen
wrestle jostle hustle

3 Write one of the words from the box above in the gaps so that the story makes sense. You may have to add a suffix to some of the words. Think carefully about this!

The c.................. was full of people. Everywhere

people were h.................. and b.................. and

j.................. one another. Suddenly a piercing

w.................. made them stop. "L..................!" called

the announcer. "The w.................. is about to begin!"

w before r

Some words that sound as if they begin with **r** have a silent **w** at the beginning.

wrong write wrote
wrap wriggle wretch
wreck wrestle wrinkle
wring wrist

4 Fill in each gap with a word beginning with **wr** to continue the story.

When the .... asked for an opponent, the

knight .... out of his armour. "You

..................!" he cried. "If you think you can escape,

you are ....!" But the .... had

strong .... He .... his arms round

the knight and tried to .... his neck.

Sssshh! Here comes the conductor!

*Who **kn**ows?*

*But what happened to the **kn**ight?*

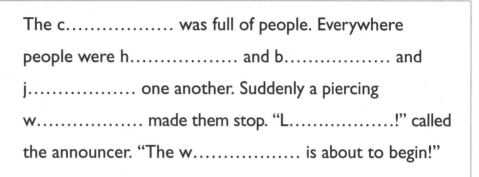

For more about silent letters, look at page 13 of your Mini Reference Book

MR

▶ s or es
▶ words ending in **y**
▶ special plurals

Singular and plural

Many happy returns!

1 On a separate piece of paper, write out the card that came with the conductor's present, making all the underlined words plural.

A **singular** word refers to one thing or one group of things. A **plural** word refers to more than one thing or more than one group of things. Most singular words can be changed to plural by adding **s** at the end.

Words ending in **s**, **sh**, **tch**, **x**, **z** would be very difficult to pronounce if they just added **s** for their plurals, so we add **es**.

pitch   pitches   box   boxes   dish   dishes
buzz   buzzes   bass   basses

Words ending in **ch** where the **ch** sounds like **tch** form their plurals with **es** as well.

speech   speech**es**

Here are the <u>polish</u> for your <u>shoe</u>. The <u>catch</u> on these <u>box</u> are very stiff. I had to use <u>wrench</u> to close them. With all good <u>wish</u> for your birthday,
Aunt Agnes

Words ending with **y** form their plurals in two ways.

If there is a vowel before the **y**, just add an **s** to form the plural.

If there is a consonant before the **y**, change the **y** to **i** and add **es**.

toy toy**s**
monkey monkey**s**
dairy dair**ies**

2 On a separate piece of paper, write out the conductor's list of birthday presents again, changing the words in brackets to their plurals.

(Toy) from Jean's (boy)
(Dish) of (toffee) from my (niece)
(Diary) from two of my (aunty)
Sugar (sweety) from the cat
Bus (pass) from admiring (lady)
Bottled (peach) from the (soprano)

Words ending in **o** or with two vowels simply add **s** to form the plural.

solo solos   piano pianos   tattoo tattoos   cuckoo cuckoos

A few singular words ending in **o** add **es** to form the plural.

potato potatoes   tomato tomatoes   echo echoes
volcano   volcanoes   mosquito   mosquitoes
tornado   tornadoes   cargo   cargoes

A few words have special ways of forming their plurals.

mouse mice   child children   man men
woman women   wife wives   life lives   shelf shelves
leaf leaves   thief thieves   loaf loaves   wolf wolves
scarf scarves   half halves   calf calves

A few words do not change at all
in their plurals.   sheep   aircraft

3 Rewrite the conductor's list of favourite birthday things on a separate piece of paper making each word plural.

> ### FAVOURITE BIRTHDAY THINGS
>
> party, child, jelly, gingerbread man, sandwich,
> candle, strawberry, parcel, speech

4 The conductor has written a song for his birthday, but the typist has put "One" at the beginning of each line instead of "No". On a separate piece of paper, correct her mistakes and change each line so that it is correct.

On the twelfth day of August,   One telephone ringing,
I wish that there could be   One piano playing,
One choir boy leaping,   One long solo,
One watch beeping,   One rustling leaf,
One double bass strumming,   One stealing thief,
One drummer drumming,   One missing box,
One lady singing,   But a peaceful birthday just for me!

For more about singular and plural, look at pages 14–15 of your Mini Reference Book

i before e
i, u and v endings
oi or oy

Useful rules

Here are some rules that are very useful if you know when **not** to use them as well as when you can.

i before e

i before **e** except immediately after **c** – when the sound is a long **e**

> receive   deceive   **BUT**   believe   retrieve   achieve   grieve

But when the vowel sound in the word is a long **a** or **i** sound, the rule is always **e** before **i**

> weigh   eight   sleigh   height

Here's the rule.

1 Write **ie** or **ei** in the gaps. Say the words out loud to help you decide.

> I have rec......ved a parcel. Its h......ght is two metres. Its w......ght is ......ght kilograms. It is ......ther a sl......gh from my n......ghbour or, I bel......ve, someone is trying to dec......ve me. That would gr......ve me very much.

E-asy endings

Hardly any English words end in **i** or **u** or **v**. If the word sounds as if it ends in **i** or **u** or **v**, there is almost certainly an **e** after those letters.

> die   lie   tie   pie
> blue   glue   rescue   true
> achieve   live   revolve   have

2 How many of the words in the list can you find in this wordsearch square?

```
T R U E U R W F
R T D L S E R J
A C H I E V E A
G T I E T O S D
L X N H C L C B
U K P A I V U L
E L I V O E E U
D I E E T Q U E
```

20

Other words that sound as if they end with **i**, really end with **y**. Many of these have two consonants before the **y**.

cry   why   try   fly   my   buy   fry   dry   guy

Exceptions are a few words that have come from other languages:

taxi   mini   ski
gnu   emu   guru

3 Fill in the spaces to complete the words. They all end with a long **i** sound.

Every night I l...... and cr......

Because I cannot t...... m...... t.......

I don't know wh....... – I really tr......!

I sometimes think that I shall d......!

Poor g......! I'll fl......

To b...... him a ready-tied bow t......!

A royal noise

If an **oy** sound comes right at the end of a word or syllable, it is always spelt **oy**. If it comes in the middle of a syllable, it is spelt **oi**.

boy   toy   royal   loyal   annoying   enjoyment
BUT noise   avoided   oil   boil   soil   moist   voice

4 Fill in the gaps with **oy** or **oi**. Be careful with plurals. Words ending with a vowel + **y** do not change their spelling when an **s** is added to form the plural.

We have a difficult ch......ce to make for the r......al

concert. Will the King enj...... hearing b......s singing a

l......al greeting or will it cause him ann......ance? That is

the p......nt. We must av......d sp......ling the whole thing.

Sounds the same

Words that sound exactly the same but have different meanings and spellings are called **homophones**. You probably know lots of these already. Making a list of new homophones as you meet them will help you to remember their different spellings.

1 On a separate piece of paper, write out the seven pairs of homophones you find in this letter.

From His Royal Highness, King Albert XXIX

Dear Sir,

I must write to offer my thanks for the great pleasure it was to hear your orchestra last night. I was almost in tears as I rose to cheer at the end. The packed tiers of seats and the rows of applauding fans showed how right you were not to meddle with our favourite tunes. Modern music can grate on the ear. It is not what we want here. At a special ceremony on Monday, I look forward to making you a knight and giving a medal to each of your players.

With thanks,

Albert R

2 Fill the gaps in the sentences with the words in brackets. If you are not sure what each word means, use a dictionary.

a I shall wear my best hat .... the .... is fine or not. (weather/whether)

b It's not ....! We each have to pay our own .... to the palace! (fair/fare)

c The royal trumpeter .... his trumpet until he was .... in the face. (blue/blew)

d The .... in your bow tie is simply .... acceptable! (not/knot)

Check your spelling skills by completing my crossword.

Down

1 A band of musicians. (9)
2 A part of the alphabet. (6)
3 They took me seriously, but I was only _____. (6)
4 Similar to elves or goblins. (4)
5 The piece requires a piano, a flute and ___ oboe. (2)
7 Sticky, chewy sweets. (7)
8 He should be _____ but he is there. (4)
10 It is red and can be used in a salad. (7)
16 She is ___ beautiful ___ a rose! (2)
17 They say you should make ___ while the sun shines. (3)
18 The most important person in an orchestra! (9)
19 A monkey. (3)
20 Another word for hate that rhymes with rise. (7)
21 I gave her my _____ for the lovely present. (6)
22 It had to ___ seen to ___ believed. (2)
24 In the winter, I wear lots of _____ of clothes. (7)
25 Some singers have beautiful _____. (6)
27 A musical instrument that you blow. (4)
28 A few, not all. (4)
32 The opposite of down. (2)

Across

1 Used to stop a bicycle wheel squeaking. (3)
6 If you have one, you want to scratch it! (4)
9 Pleasure. (9)
11 A knife can do this. (3)
12 I shall accept the King's _____ of a knighthood. (5)
13 His trumpet has lost ___ shine. (3)
14 Every one of these in my orchestra is highly trained. (6)
15 What something is if it is not bent. (8)
19 King John reigned long ___. (3)
21 If at first you don't succeed, you must do this again and again. (3)
23 He told dreadful lies, but I _____ him. (8)
26 The cat was shut in a cupboard, but I helped him to _____. (6)
28 They ____ that I am a genius. (3)
29 What you should do if a gnat flies towards your eye! (5)
30 A small, furry pet that catches mice. (3)
31 A boat that travels under the water. (9)
33 A number that is not odd is ____. (4)
34 Everyone should call me this! (3)

 Keep your Mini Reference Book handy to help you with spelling.

Spelling strategies

Here are some tips to help you with spelling.

1 To learn to spell a new word, or an old one that is giving you trouble, follow these steps:

- ▶ **Look** carefully at the word, thinking about how its parts fit together.
- ▶ **Say** the word out loud a few times, looking closely at how it is spelt.
- ▶ **Write** the word several times in your usual handwriting. Notice how it feels to write the word and the shape that it makes.
- ▶ **Cover** your writing and write the word again without looking. Spell it aloud as you write it.
- ▶ **Check** that you have spelt the word correctly.

2 When you are reading and meet new words, look out for word patterns. Notice if the word has a prefix or suffix and whether it uses the same spelling pattern as a word you already know.

3 Try working out your own **mnemonic** (the m is silent). That is a way of remembering something. For example, you could remember how to spell island by saying:

An island **is land** with water all round it.

4 When you are writing something important, write it out in rough first and use a dictionary to look up any words you are not sure about. Then write a neat copy.

5 Whether you have made a rough version first or not, always read through your writing when you have finished. Is there anything that looks a little odd and should be checked?

Practice makes perfect!

Purrrrr-fect!

6 Have fun with words by doing wordsearches or crosswords, and playing Scrabble or other games. Any game where you have to look carefully at words will help with spelling.